Bible Question Class Books

Bible Study Questions on
The Book of 2 Samuel
by David E. Pratte

A workbook suitable for Bible classes,
family studies, or personal Bible study

Available in print at
www.gospelway.com/sales

Bible Study Questions on the Book of 2 Samuel:
A workbook suitable for Bible classes, family studies,
or personal Bible study

ISBN-13: 978-1981367504
ISBN-10: 1981367500

Printed books, booklets, and tracts available at
www.gospelway.com/sales
Free Bible study articles online at
www.gospelway.com
Free Bible courses online at
www.biblestudylessons.com
Free class books at
www.biblestudylessons.com/classbooks
Free commentaries on Bible books at
www.biblestudylessons.com/commentary
Contact the author at
www.gospelway.com/comments

Note carefully: No teaching in any of our materials is intended or should ever be construed to justify or to in any way incite or encourage personal vengeance or physical violence against any person.

"He who glories, let him glory in the Lord"
– 1 Corinthians 1:31

Front Page Photo

The Tell Dan Steele, discovered in 1993/1994, describes a battle in which the Syrians fought against the king of Israel; they claim to have defeated the house of David. Although this refers to a battle after the time of David himself, it does refer to the house of David, which is an expression used nearly two dozen times in the Scriptures to refer to David's dynasty.

Photo credit: Oren Rozen distributed under creative commons license or GNU free documentation license, via Wikimedia Commons

Other Books by the Author

Topical Bible Studies

Growing a Godly Marriage & Raising Godly Children
Why Believe in God, Jesus, and the Bible? (evidences)
The God of the Bible (study of the Father, Son, and Holy Spirit)
Grace, Faith, and Obedience: The Gospel or Calvinism?
Kingdom of Christ: Future Millennium or Present Spiritual Reign?
Do Not Sin Against the Child: Abortion, Unborn Life, & the Bible
True Words of God: Bible Inspiration and Preservation

Commentaries on Bible Books

Genesis	*Gospel of John*
Joshua and Ruth	*Acts*
Judges	*Romans*
1 Samuel	*Ephesians*
2 Samuel	*Philippians and Colossians*
Ezra, Nehemiah, and Esther	*Hebrews*
Job	*James and Jude*
Proverbs	*1 & 2 Peter*
Gospel of Mark	

Bible Question Class Books

Genesis	*Gospel of Luke*
Joshua and Ruth	*Gospel of John*
Judges	*Acts*
1 Samuel	*Romans*
2 Samuel	*1 Corinthians*
Ezra, Nehemiah, and Esther	*2 Corinthians and Galatians*
Job	*Ephesians and Philippians*
Proverbs	*Colossians, 1&2 Thessalonians*
Ecclesiastes	*1 & 2 Timothy, Titus, Philemon*
Isaiah	*Hebrews*
Gospel of Matthew	*General Epistles (James - Jude)*
Gospel of Mark	*Revelation*

Workbooks with Study Notes

Jesus Is Lord: Workbook on the Fundamentals of the Gospel of Christ
Following Jesus: Workbook on Discipleship
God's Eternal Purpose in Christ: Workbook on the Theme of the Bible

The Family Reading Booklist

Visit our website at www.gospelway.com/sales **to see a current list of books in print.**

Bible Study Questions on the Book of 2 Samuel

Introduction:

This workbook was designed for Bible class study, family study, or personal study. The class book is suitable for teens and up. The questions contain minimal human commentary, but instead urge students to study to understand Scripture.

Enough questions are included for teachers to assign as many questions as they want for each study session. Studies may proceed at whatever speed and depth will best accomplish the needs of the students.

Questions labeled "think" are intended to encourage students to apply what they have learned. When questions refer to a map, students should consult maps in a Bible dictionary or similar reference work or in the back of their Bibles. (Note: My abbreviation "*b/c/v*" means "book, chapter, and verse.")

For class instruction, I urge teachers to assign the questions as homework so students come to class prepared. Then let class time consist of *discussion* that focuses on the Scriptures themselves. Let the teacher use other Scriptures, questions, applications, and comments to promote productive discussion, not just reading the questions to see whether they were answered "correctly." Please, do *not* let the class period consist primarily of the following: "Joe, will you answer number 1?" "Sue, what about number 2?" Etc.

I also urge students to emphasize the *Bible* teaching. Please, do not become bogged down over "What did the author mean by question #5?" My meaning is relatively unimportant. The issue is what the Bible says. Concentrate on the meaning and applications of Scripture. If a question helps promote Bible understanding, stay with it. If it becomes unproductive, move on.

The questions are not intended just to help students understand the Scriptures. They are also designed to help students learn good principles of Bible study. Good Bible study requires defining the meaning of keywords, studying parallel passages, explaining the meaning of the text clearly, making applications, and defending the truth as well as exposing religious error. I have included questions to encourage students to practice all these study principles.

Finally, I encourage plain applications of the principles studied. God's word is written so souls may please God and have eternal life. Please study it with the respect and devotion it deserves!

For whatever good this material achieves, to God be the glory.

Bible study commentary and notes to accompany this and other of our workbooks are available at www.gospelway.com/sales

© David E. Pratte, January 4, 2018

Workbooks, commentaries, and topical studies for sale in print at www.gospelway.com/sales

To join our mailing list to be informed of new books or special sales, contact the author at www.gospelway.com/comments

---

Assignments on 2 Samuel 1

Read 2 Samuel 1, then answer the following questions. If you need help, consult a Bible dictionary or similar reference work.

1. Skim the book of 2 Samuel and summarize its theme.

2. ***Special Assignment:*** What you can learn about the inspired author of the book?

3. Describe how the book of 2 Samuel relates to the books of 1 Samuel, 1 Kings, and 1 Chronicles.

4. What was the slaughter of the Amalekites mentioned in 1:1? Describe what happened and why.

5. Where was David at this time (see ***map***)? Why was David there rather than at the battle against the Philistines (study the account in 1 Samuel)?

6. Describe the man who came to David and tell how he acted – 1:2.

7. What did David ask, and what information did the man give – 1:3,4?

8. Explain how these events relate to the end of the book of 1 Samuel.

9. Describe the account the man gave of the death of Saul – 1:5-10.

10. How does this man's story differ from the account given in 1 Samuel 31? (Note the man's nationality – verse 8.)

---

11. **Special Assignment:** What possibilities can you suggest to explain the differences between this man's account and 1 Samuel 31?

---

12. How did David and his men respond to the news of the battle – 1:11,12? (Think: Why would they so respond?)

13. What questions did David ask the messenger in 1:13,14?

14. What command did David give regarding the messenger, and what reason did he give – 1:15,16?

---

15. **Application**: How did David's reactions here compared to his earlier attitudes toward Saul? What lessons should we learn about our attitudes toward people in authority?

---

16. What information is found in 1:17-27? What did David want to be done with it? (Think: Why is it called the song of the Bow?

17. What did David say in 1:19 had happened? How did he describe those who had died?

18. Where did he not want this information to be made known – 1:20? Explain why not.

19. What did David say about Gilboa in 1:21? Why would he say this and how was Gilboa involved in the story? (Think: Try to explain the references to shields.)

20. How did he describe Jonathan and Saul as warriors in 1:22?

21. What were Jonathan and Saul like in their lives and in their death – 1:23? Explain the reference to eagles and lions.

22. What had Saul done for the daughters of Israel – 1:24? So what should they do now?

23. What expression is repeated in 1:25,27? Where else had it been used earlier?

24. How did David describe his relationship with Jonathan – 1:25,26?

25. List other *passages* that describe the closeness between David and Jonathan.

26. *Application*: What admirable qualities did Jonathan show in his relationship to David? What can we learn from his example?

27. How did David conclude his song of mourning – 1:27?

Assignments on 2 Samuel 2

Read 2 Samuel 2, then answer the following questions.

1. What questions did David ask the Lord – 2:1? What answers did he receive? (Think: Why would David need to ask such questions of the Lord?)

2. Where did David go and who went with him – 2:2,3 (see **map**)?

3. **Special Assignment:** What method would David have used to ask these questions of the Lord (study similar examples in the book of 1 Samuel)?

4. Who anointed David as king – 2:4? (Think: Why would they have done this before Israel did? Who had already anointed David as king?)

5. What information was David given in 2:4? Where else is the story recorded? Give more details about what happened.

6. What did David say to these people as a result – 2:5,6? (Think: Why would these men have been the ones to have done this?)

7. What challenge did David give these people in 2:7?

8. Who had been the commander of Saul's army – 2:8? What did he do that was destined to lead to conflict with David – 2:8,9? Where was this done (see **map**)?

9. **Special Assignment:** What responsibility would Saul have had in the conflict that resulted? What can we learn about our relationships in the church?

10. How old was Ishbosheth, and how long did he reign – 2:10,11? How long did David reign over Judah in Hebron?

11. Describe how open hostility between David's household and Saul's household began – 2:12-16. Where did this occur (see **map**)?

12. Explain the purpose of such a contest. What was the outcome in this case?

13. Rather than the conflict being resolved by the contest of the young men, what followed – 2:17? What was the outcome?

14. How many sons did Zeruiah have in the battle and what were their names – 2:18? (Think: Who was Zeruiah?)

15. What characteristic did Asahel have, and how did he use his ability – 2:18,19?

16. What did Abner urge Asahel to do – 2:20,21? What was the result?

17. What reason did Abner give to persuade Asahel – 2:22? (Think: Why might Abner be concerned about Joab?)

18. What did Abner finally do about Asahel – 2:23?

19. As the pursuit continued, what did Abner's followers do – 2:24,25?

20. What request did Abner make of Joab – 2:26?

21. **Special Assignment:** State your evaluation of Abner's advice. Was Abner himself in any way responsible for the bitterness and conflict?

22. How did Joab respond to Abner and what was the result – 2:27,28?

23. Where did Abner and his men go then – 2:29?

24. What further information is given about the battle in 2:30,31?

25. **Special Assignment:** How would you compare the number of casualties in this battle to other battles the Israelites fought? Aside from the numbers, what significance did this battle have in the conflict between David's followers and Saul's followers?

26. What did Joab's men do regarding Asahel – 2:32? Where were they from?

27. Where did Joab's men go then?

Assignments on 2 Samuel 3

Read 2 Samuel 3, then answer the following questions.

1. What followed from the events in chapter 2 – 3:1? How are the results described?

2. List the sons of David who were born in Hebron – 3:2-5. For each one, briefly tell what other information you have about them.

3. What did Abner accomplish as the war continued – 3:6?

4. Why was Ishbosheth upset with Abner – 3:7? (Think: Consider what significance Abner's act would have regarding his authority in the kingdom.)

5. How did Abner respond to Ishbosheth – 3:8?

6. What promise did Abner then make to Ishbosheth – 3:9-11? How did Ishbosheth respond and why? (Think: Why would this be significant in the conflict?)

7. **Application**: What statement did Abner make in verse 9 about David's reign? What does this show about Abner's own conduct? What lessons should we learn?

8. What offer did Abner make to David in 3:12?

9. How did David respond and what condition did he require – 3:13? Who was Michal, and why would David make this request?

Workbook on 2 Samuel

10. What demand did David then make of Ishbosheth? What was the result – 3:14-16?

11. What did Abner then urge the elders of Israel to do – 3:17,18? What did he once again acknowledge that he knew about David?

12. What information did Abner then report to David – 3:19? Why would Abner especially need to speak to the people of Benjamin?

13. Describe the meeting between Abner and David – 3:20. Who went with Abner, and how did David treat them?

14. What promise did Abner make to David – 3:21? How did David respond?

15. Where had Joab been, and what did he learn when he returned – 3:22,23?

16. What accusation did Joab make to David about Abner – 3:24,25? (Think: Was Joab motivated entirely by concern for David and the nation? Explain.)

17. For what purpose did Joab send messengers – 3:26? (Think: Why might he not have told David?)

18. Describe the death of Abner – 3:27.

19. **Special Assignment:** What motivated Joab in this act (see also verse 30)? Was he justified in what he did? Why or why not?

20. How did David view responsibility for this act – 3:28,29?

21. What consequence did David call for on the house of Joab?

22. Describe the funeral of Abner – 3:31,32. (Think: How was this a rebuke to Joab?)

23. In his lamentation, how did David describe the death of Abner – 3:33,34?

24. What did the people then ask David to do, and how did he respond – 3:35?

25. What did the people think and what did they understand as result of David's conduct – 3:36,37?

26. *Application*: Why would it be important to David for the people to understand how he viewed the death of Abner? What lessons should we learn?

27. How did David describe Abner to his servants – 3:38?

28. What reason did David give why he had not punished the sons of Zeruiah – 3:39? (Think: Was David's reaction adequate considering the wrong that had been done?)

29. Whom did David say would repay the evildoer? Study cross references and see who eventually was responsible to punish Joab.

Assignments on 2 Samuel 4

Read 2 Samuel 4, then answer the following questions.

1. What reactions resulted from Abner's death– 4:1? Why would these people react in this way?

2. What two men are introduced in 4:2,3? What are we told about them?

3. What man is introduced in 4:4? What problem did he have, and what had caused it? (Think: How does this man enter into the story later?)

4. Describe the death of Ishbosheth – 4:5-7.

5. What did the assassins do after Ishbosheth's death – 4:8? (Think: What were they probably expecting from David?)

6. What previous event did David recall to these men – 4:9,10?

7. What application did David make to the assassins – 4:11? (Think: In what sense was Ishbosheth righteous?)

8. What reward did David give the assassins – 4:12?

9. What respect did David show to Ishbosheth?

10. **Application**: What can we learn about our conduct toward others from examples like this in the life of David?

Assignments on 2 Samuel 5

Read 2 Samuel 5, then answer the following questions.

1. What reasons did the tribes of Israel give for following David – 5:1,2?

2. What did the elders do as a result – 5:3?

3. How old was David when he began to reign, and how long did he reign – 5:4? How long over Judah, and how long over all Israel and Judah – 5:5?

4. What city did David want to capture, and what did the inhabitants of that city say about it – 5:6? (Think: Why might they have said this?)

5. What promise did David make to motivate his army? What was the result – 5:7,8?

6. Who led the attack and what happened as result – 1 Chronicles 11:6?

7. What did David then do with the city – 5:9?

8. What did David accomplish following this? Why was he able to do so – 5:10?

9. Who did a favor for David, and what did he do – 5:11? (Think: What does this show us about this man?)

10. What did these events lead David to realize – 5:12?

11. As David increased in power, what else increased – 5:13?

12. List the names of the sons born to David in Jerusalem – 5:14-16.

13. ***Special Assignment:*** What had God warned kings about in Deuteronomy 17:17? Explain why this would be a problem. How does David's family demonstrate this?

14. Who then became a danger, and what did they do – 5:17,18?

15. What did David do before the battle, and what promise did he receive – 5:19?

16. What was the result of the battle – 5:20? What name did David give as a result?

17. What did the enemy leave behind, and what did David's army do with them – 5:21? According to 1 Chronicles 14:12, what else did they do?

18. What did the Philistines do next, and what guidance did David receive – 5:22-24?

19. What was the outcome of this battle – 5:25 (see ***map***)? What effect did this have for David according to 1 Chronicles 14:17?

20. ***Application***: What lessons can we learn from the fact that David consulted with God before each battle?

Assignments on 2 Samuel 6

Read 2 Samuel 6, then answer the following questions.

1. Who gathered together and what was their purpose – 6:1,2? (See also 2 Chronicles 13. Find another name for the place where they went. See a *map*.)

2. ***Special Assignment:*** Explain how the ark came to be in this place (1 Samuel 4-7). (Think: What is the significance of the terms used to describe God in verse 2?)

3. Who transported the ark, and how did they do it – 6:3,4?

4. List other ***passages*** and explain how the ark was supposed to be transported.

5. How did David and the people accompany this event – 6:5?

6. As the ark was moving, what happened, and what was the consequence – 6:6,7?

7. ***Application***: Explain the mistake that David and the people made. What lessons should we learn? Are all religious acts acceptable, especially if done sincerely or with good intentions? List modern examples in which religious people make similar mistakes.

8. How did David react to this event, and what did he name the place – 6:8?

9. What concerns did David have in 6:9? (Think: Answer David's question.)

10. What did David then do with the ark – 6:10? (Think: What else can you learn about this man?)

11. How long was the ark in the house of Obed-Edom, and how was he treated as a result – 6:11?

12. What did David do then – 6:12?

---

13. **Special Assignment:** Study 1 Chronicles 15 and explain why David was successful this time in transported the ark. What can we learn?

---

14. As they began transporting the ark, what did David do – 6:13?

15. How did David and the people celebrate this event – 6:14,15?

16. Who did not share David's enthusiasm? What did she do – 6:16? (Think: What might have changed her attitude toward David?)

17. What did David do when the ark arrived – 6:17-19?

18. What criticism was raised against David when he returned home – 6:20? (Think: Had David done anything wrong? What might have contributed to the criticism? Explain.)

19. What response did David give to the criticism – 6:21,22?

20. What consequence came upon Michal – 6:23? (Think: What difficulty is found regarding this in other passages? What may possibly explain the difficulty?)

Assignments on 2 Samuel 7

Read 2 Samuel 7, then answer the following questions.

1. What concern did David express to Nathan in 7:1,2? (Think: According to the context, what did he intend to do about this?)

2. How did Nathan respond to David – 7:3?

3. **Application**: What lessons might we learn about caring for the place where we worship God compared to caring for our own homes?

4. According to 7:4-6, what did God realize that David wanted to do? What did God say about living in a tent?

5. What question had God not asked the people – 7:7? (Think: Is God saying here that David wanted to do something unscriptural? How do you know?)

6. According to 1 Chronicles 17:4; 22:6-10, who did God say would and would not build His house, and what reasons did He give?

7. What blessings had God given David according to 7:8,9?

8. What did God promise to do for Israel in 7:10,11?

9. What did God promise to do for David – 7:11-13? What kind of house did He mean?

10. List other **passages** that help explain the fulfillment of God's promise to David.

11. **Special Assignment:** Explain how the promise to David is fulfilled in Jesus and in the church. Is the church a political kingdom or spiritual kingdom? Consider John 18:36; Matthew 16:18,19; Mark 9:1; Acts 1:3-8; chapter 2; Colossians 1:13,14; Revelation 1:9; etc.

12. What did God promise to do for David's seed in 7:14-17?

13. What can we learn about the significance of David's throne from passages such as Psalm 110:1-4; Zechariah 6:12,13; Acts 2:30-36; Hebrews 8:1?

14. Having received this promise from God, what did David do – 7:18-20? How did David view himself in light of God's promise?

15. What reason did David give why God had done these things – 7:21?

16. What conclusion did David reach about God – 7:22? What lessons should we learn about our blessings?

17. What did David say God had done for Israel – 7:23,24?

18. So what prayer or request did David make in 7:25,26?

19. What reason did David give why he had prayed this prayer – 7:27?

20. What reason did David have for believing that the promise would come true – 7:28,29?

Assignments on 2 Samuel 8

Read 2 Samuel 8, then answer the following questions.

1. Against which nation did David fight in 8:1? What was the result?

2. Whom did he defeat in 8:2? How did he treat them? (Think: Was David normally this cruel to his enemies?)

3. Whom did David fight in 8:3,4? (See **map**.) What was the result? Why did David so treat the horses (see Deuteronomy 17:16)?

4. Who then joined the battle – 8:5,6? What was the result?

5. Describe the spoil that David took – 8:7,8.

6. Who acted peaceably towards David? What did he do – 8:9,10? (See **map**.)

7. What did David do with the spoil that he had received – 8:11,12 (see also 1 Chronicles 18)? What can we learn from this about David?

8. Whom else did David fight, and what was the result – 8:13,14?

9. **Special Assignment:** What reason does the account give for David's success – see verses 6, 14? Why is this important to remember?

10. List the various officers who served under David – 8:15-18. What do we know about some of them?

Assignments on 2 Samuel 9

Read 2 Samuel 9, then answer the following questions.

1. What concern did David have according to 9:1? Why would David have this concern?

2. List other **passages** that explain David's attitude towards Jonathan.

3. Whom did David find to help him, and what information did he receive – 9:2,3?

4. Where was this son of Jonathan – 9:4,5? (See **map.**)

5. What was the son's name – 9:6? How did he greet David?

6. What promise did David make to him – 9:7,8? How did he react?

7. Explain the significance of David's promise. Why would this be an honor?

8. What responsibility did David give to Ziba – 9:9-11? Whom did he have to help him?

9. What further information is given about Mephibosheth in 9:12,13?

10. **Application**: What can we learn about David from this story? What lessons should we learn?

Assignments on 2 Samuel 10

Read 2 Samuel 10, then answer the following questions.

1. According to 10:1,2, what king died? Who took his place?

2. Where else have we read of a battle with a king of a similar name? What was the outcome of that battle?

3. What did David decide to do, and why did he do it?

4. What motive did the princes of Ammon attribute to David – 10:3?

5. What did the king do as a result – 10:4? (Think: Why would he do this, and what affect would it have on David?)

6. What did David say to his messengers, and why – 10:5?

7. **Application**: What can we learn and what application can we make even today about wearing short garments?

8. List other **passages** about making false accusations against others.

9. **Application**: What can we learn and what application should we make about falsely attributing motives to others? Give examples.

10. What did the Ammonites do for protection, and how did David respond – 10:6,7? Locate some of the places mentioned on a *map*.

11. As the battle loomed, what problem did Joab see that he had – 10:8,9?

12. How did Joab respond to this problem – 10:9-11?

13. What encouragement did he give to his brother in 10:12? How did this demonstrate Joab's faith?

14. What was the outcome of the battle – 10:13,14? Where did Joab go afterward?

15. How did the Syrians react to this defeat – 10:15,16?

16. Who was their leader? Where did they gather (see *map*)?

17. What did David do then – 10:17? Where else is a similar battle recorded?

18. What was the outcome of this battle – 10:18?

19. How did the Syrians react to the defeat – 10:19?

Assignments on 2 Samuel 11

Read 2 Samuel 11, then answer the following questions.

1. When did the events in this chapter occur – 11:1? What did David send the army to do? Where was David at the time?

2. What did David see one evening – 11:2? Where was David when he saw this?

---

3. **Application**: What can we learn from this story about temptation?

---

4. List other **passages** about proper clothing, modesty, chastity, nakedness, etc.

---

5. **Application**: Did Bathsheeba have any responsibility in what happened? Explain. What can we learn about proper clothing?

---

6. List other **passages** about the use of rooftops in Bible times. (Think: Was David wrong to be on his rooftop?)

7. What inquiry did David make, and what answer was he given – 11:3? What should this information have led him to do?

8. What did David do and what happened as result – 11:4? (Think: What is the significance of the fact that she was cleansed from her impurity?)

9. What message did Bathsheeba send to David – 11:5? Why was this a complication?

10. What was the penalty for adultery under the Law? Give book/chapter/verse.

11. What message did David send to Joab – 11:6,7? What did David inquire of Uriah?

12. What did David then suggest that Uriah do – 11:8? What would David's purpose have been in suggesting this?

13. What did Uriah do instead – 11:9? Why would this be a problem for David?

14. What did David ask Uriah, and what was the response – 11:10,11?

15. What plan did David pursue then – 11:12,13? What was the result?

16. What do these events show us about the character of Uriah? (Think: How does this make David's conduct even more objectionable?)

17. What message did David then send to Joab, and how did he send it – 11:14,15? What would have been David's intent in this?

18. **Application**: What can we learn from these events about the progressive nature of sin – that is, how does sin often lead people deeper and deeper into further sin?

19. What did Joab do in response to David's instructions? What resulted – 11:16,17?

20. How did Joab then communicate with David – 11:18-20? What question did he expect that David might ask?

21. What event might David recall – 11:21? What Scripture records the story?

22. What was the messenger to say if David brought this up? Why would this response satisfy David?

23. What can we learn from this story about the character of Joab?

24. How did the messenger describe the battle to David 11:22-24?

25. What message did David then send back to Joab – 11:25?

26. **Application**: David had Bathsheeba's husband murdered in order to cover up the fact they conceived out of wedlock. What solution do many people in our society seek if they conceive out of wedlock? What lessons can we learn?

27. What did Bathsheeba do when she heard of the death of Uriah – 7:26?

28. What happened after the days of mourning were over – 11:27?

29. How does the passage describe God's view of the event. Explain why God would view it this way?

30. **Application**: Compare how the Bible views this story to the way the modern entertainment industry would portray it.

Workbook on 2 Samuel

Assignments on 2 Samuel 12

Read 2 Samuel 12, then answer the following questions.

1. List other **passages** about the need for sin to be rebuked.

2. **Application**: Describe some advantages of using parables like Nathan did.

3. In your own words, tell the story that Nathan told to David – 12:1-4.

4. **Special Assignment:** Describe how Nathan's story was like David's case.

5. What was David's reaction to the story – 12:5,6? What reasons did he give?

6. List other **passages** about the concept of restitution.

7. Explain the Bible concept of restitution.

8. How did Nathan make the application to David – 12:7?

9. What did God say that He had done for David – 12:7,8?

10. How did Nathan describe David's sin in 12:9?

11. **Application**: In what sense was it true that David killed Uriah? What are ways people might be guilty of a sin without physically doing it?

12. What consequences did Nathan say would come upon David – 12:10-12?

13. In what sense was it true that David had despised God?

14. In what sense was this a turning point in David's life? What can we learn about the consequences of sin?

15. What confession did David make and how did Nathan respond – 12:13?

16. What consequence did Nathan say would still occur – 12:14?

17. List other *passages* about the need to repent of sins.

18. List other *passages* about the importance of godly sorrow.

19. List other *passages* about the need for an erring child of God to confess sin.

20. **Application**: What should we learn from David about how we should deal with our own sins as children of God?

21. **Application**: What did Nathan mean when he said David gave the enemies of God occasion to blaspheme? What should we learn?

22. Explain the sense in which there may be consequences for sin even after it has been forgiven.

23. How did David respond when the baby became ill – 12:15-17?

24. Why were David's servants afraid to tell him when the baby died – 12:18?

25. What did he do when the baby did die – 12:19,20?

26. What did he say when his servants questioned his response – 12:21-23?

27. **Application**: What does David's response show about the state of the dead?

28. What happened then between David and Bathsheeba – 12:24,25? What was the baby named?

29. What message did Joab send to David and why – 12:26-28?

30. Was the outcome of the battle – 12:29-31?

Assignments on 2 Samuel 13

Read 2 Samuel 13, then answer the following questions.

1. Describe the four main characters in this story:

Absalom –

Tamar –

Amnon –

Jonadab –

2. How did Amnon feel about Tamar – 13:1,2? Why did he not pursue his feelings?

3. *Application*: Was Amnon's feeling truly love in the Biblical sense? What should we learn about the difference between love and lust?

4. What kind of man was Jonadab? What question did he ask, and what was the answer – 13:3,4?

5. What suggestion did Jonadab give – 13:5? (Think: Did this make sense as a legitimate cure for Amnon?)

6. *Application*: What should we learn about the importance of the friends that we choose? List other *passages*.

7. So what request did Amnon make, and how did David respond – 13:6,7?

8. What did Tamar do? What instructions did Amnon give then – 13:8-10?

9. *Application*: What lessons should we learn about an unmarried man and woman being alone in a bedroom?

10. What demand did Amnon make then – 13:11? (Think: At this point was he trying to force her or was he seeking her consent?)

11. How did Tamar respond and what reasons did she give – 13:12,13?

---

12. **Special Assignment:** Discuss Tamar's reasons for refusing. Were these good responses to the temptation?

---

13. What did Amnon do when Tamar objected – 13:14?

14. What did Amnon think of Tamar afterwards – 13:15? What did he say to her?

15. What did Tamar say to Amnon then – 13:16? Why would she say that? Give Scripture that explains her answer.

---

16. **Application**: What does Amnon's response illustrate about the results of sin? What lessons should we learn?

---

17. What did Amnon do regarding Tamar then – 13:17,18?

18. How did Tamar express her grief – 13:19?

19. What advice did Absalom give Tamar in 13:20? (Think: Why should the fact that she was wronged by a brother lead Tamar to keep quiet?)

20. How did David feel when he heard – 13:21?

21. ***Application***: Did David deal with this situation properly? Explain. What should we learn?

22. How did Absalom view what Amnon had done – 13:22?

23. What event gave Absalom an opportunity for revenge – 13:23,24? Who all had been invited?

24. Whom did Absalom want to attend when David refused – 13:25-27?

25. What instruction did Absalom give his servants and what was the result – 13:28,29?

26. What news came to David and how did he respond – 13:30,31? What should we learn about believing falsehoods?

27. Who corrected the misinformation David had received – 13:32-35? What did he say?

28. Nevertheless, how did the king and his sons and servants react – 13:36?

29. Where did Absalom go and how long did he stay – 13:37,38? Why would he have gone there (see ***map***)?

30. ***Special Assignment:*** How did David feel about Absalom then – 13:39? What responsibility did David have in all these sad events?

Assignments on 2 Samuel 14

Read 2 Samuel 14, then answer the following questions.

1. What did Joab realize about David – 14:1? (Think: How did this relate to the events of chapter 13?)

2. What did Joab ask a woman to do – 14:2,3? (Find Tekoa on a *map*.)

3. When the woman went to David, what did he ask her, and how did she describe herself – 14:4,5?

4. Describe the story that she told about her sons – 14:6,7.

5. What problem would this have caused for the woman?

6. *Special Assignment:* In what way was the story the woman described like David's case with Absalom? In what way was it different? (Think: Was Absalom next in line for the throne, and how might this affect the situation?)

7. What commitment did David make in 14:8? Explain her response in 14:9.

8. What assurance did the woman want in 14:10,11, and what did David promise?

9. *Special Assignment:* Explain the Old Testament law of the manslayer and give Scripture for your answer.

10. How would this law affect the case of the woman's sons, and how would it affect the case of Absalom?

11. What application did the woman make to David – 14:12,13?

12. Explain how 14:14 applies to the situation.

13. What reason did she give why she came to David – 14:15-17?

14. What question did David ask the woman and how did she respond – 14:18-20?

15. What decision did David make – 14:21,22?

16. What restriction did David place on Absalom when he returned – 14:23,24? (Think: What purpose would this restriction accomplish?)

17. Describe Absalom according to 14:25,26? What did the people think of him? (Think: what does this tell us about Absalom?)

18. What information is given about Absalom's family – 14:27?

19. What request did Absalom make of Joab, and what did he do to get Joab to comply – 14:28-31?

20. What concern did Absalom want Joab to express to David – 14:32? (Think: Was his request reasonable? Explain.)

21. What was the end result – 14:33?

Assignments on 2 Samuel 15

Read 2 Samuel 15, then answer the following questions.

1. How did Absalom choose to travel – 15:1? What was the purpose?

2. What did he do for people who came to the king for judgment – 15:2-4?

3. If Absalom was really concerned about better justice for the people, what could he have done to help David?

4. How did Absalom treat people according to 15:5?

5. What effect did all this have on the people – 15:6?

6. *Application*: What is the motive for the kind of conduct in which Absalom engaged? Give examples in which people sometimes act similarly today.

7. Where did Absalom want to go – 15:7-9? What reason did he give to David?

8. What role had Hebron played in Absalom's history and David's history? (Think: How might this have entered into Absalom's plans?)

9. What did Absalom do then that showed his real intentions – 15:10?

10. Who went with Absalom, and what was their intention – 15:11?

11. **Special Assignment:** What do these events show about Absalom's character?

12. Who joined Absalom's conspiracy – 15:12? How would this help Absalom's plans?

13. What message did David receive, and what did he decide to do – 15:13,14?

14. Who went with David – 15:15-18? What do you know about these people?

15. Whom did David leave behind, and for what purpose?

16. What man followed David and what reason did he give him to return – 15:19,20?

17. What response did this man give to David – 15:21,22? What can we learn about him from this?

18. **Special Assignment:** From what city had this man come (study the word "Gittite")? What connection had David had with this place in his past history?

19. How did the people proceed – 15:23? How far had they gone (see **map**)?

20. Who then met David and what was with them – 15:24? (Think: Why might this have been valuable to David?)

21. What instruction did David give the priests – 15:25,26?

22. What reason did David give the priests? In what way was his attitude admirable?

23. What additional purpose did David say the priests could accomplish – 15:27-29?

24. What place had David reached then (see a **map**) – 15:30? What else do you know about this place?

25. How is the people's conduct described in verse 30? What is the significance?

26. What information was David given, and how did he respond – 15:31?

27. What did David do at the top of the mountain – 15:32? What can we learn?

28. Who met David there? How was he expressing grief?

29. What did David advise him to do – 15:33,34? For what purpose?

30. With whom could Hushai work – 15:35-37? What arrangements did David urge?

Assignments on 2 Samuel 16

Read 2 Samuel 16, then answer the following questions.

1. Who came to David then, and what did he bring – 16:1?

2. What purpose did he say his gift would serve – 16:2?

3. What did David ask him, and what was the answer – 16:3?

4. What decision did David make based on this information – 16:4? (Think: We will see this turns out not to be true. What lessons can we learn?)

5. What man confronted David next and of whose family was he – 16:5?

6. What did he do and what accusations did he make against David – 16:6-8?

7. *Special Assignment:* In what ways did these accusations differ from the truth? (Think: What might have motivated such false accusations?)

8. Who wanted to respond, and what did he want to do – 16:9?

9. What did David say should be done and why – 16:10,11?

10. What good did David hope might come – 16:12,13?

11. **Special Assignment:** How did these events relate to David's sin and the punishment that God had decreed? In what sense was God behind these events?

12. **Application**: God had decreed punishments for both Saul and David for their sins. Compare their reactions to the punishments. What lessons can we learn?

13. Compare the circumstances of David to that of Absalom at this point – 16:14,15.

14. How did Hushai greet Absalom – 16:16? (Think: Was this sincere?)

15. What did Absalom ask him – 16:17?

16. What reason did Hushai give for being loyal to Absalom – 16:18,19?

17. What did Absalom request of Ahithophel – 16:20? (Think: Why would Absalom seek advice at this point?

18. What answer did he receive – 16:21?

19. What purpose would this serve?

20. Describe the importance of Ahithophel in the kingdom – 16:23.

Assignments on 2 Samuel 17

Read 2 Samuel 17, then answer the following questions.

1. What did Ahithophel advise Absalom to do next – 17:1?

2. What reasons did he give for this advice – 17:2,3?

3. Who else was called and what was he asked – 17:4-6?

4. How did Hushai describe David and his men – 17:7,8?

5. Why did he say Ahithophel's advice would not work, and what did he say would happen if Ahithophel's advice was followed – 17:8-10?

6. Describe the advice that Hushai gave instead – 17:11-13.

7. ***Special Assignment:*** Whose advice was really better here? Why did Hushai give the advice that he gave?

8. Whose advice was followed, and what was the real reason – 17:14?

9. What did Hushai do with the information he had – 17:15

10. What advice did he give to David – 17:16? Why?

11. Who carried the information to David – 17:17? Where were they staying and why?

12. Who carried the information to them but what went wrong – 17:17,18?

13. How were they hidden – 17:18,19?

14. Who questioned the woman and what did she say – 17:20?

15. What success did the messengers have, and what was the result – 17:20-22?

16. What did Ahithophel do when his advice had been rejected – 17:23? (Think: Why might he have gone to such an extreme?)

17. **Application:** List other Bible examples of suicide. What can we learn about suicide from these examples?

18. Where did David go (see **map**), and what did Absalom do – 17:24?

19. Who became captain of the army of Absalom and what do we know about him – 17:25? (Think: What relationship would this make him to David?)

20. Who came to David's aid, and what did they supply – 17:27-29? What else do we know about these men?

Assignments on 2 Samuel 18

Read 2 Samuel 18, then answer the following questions.

1. Describe how David organized his army – 18:1,2.

2. What plan of David did the people oppose – 18:2-4? What reason did they give? (Think: Who was right: David or the people? Why?)

3. What instruction did David give regarding Absalom – 18:5?

4. **Special Assignment:** Would David have given this instruction if the rebellion was led by someone other than one of his sons? What does this reveal about David?

5. Describe how the battle progressed – 18:6-8. How many people died? (Think: What does this reveal about the consequences of sin?)

6. What strange event occurred to Absalom in the battle – 18:9? (Think: What connection might this have had to Absalom's vanity?)

7. What did a man tell Joab about this, and how did Joab respond – 18:10,11?

8. What reason did the man give for his conduct – 18:12,13?

9. Describe Absalom's death – 18:14,15.

10. **Special Assignment:** What does this reveal about Joab?

11. What did Joab do after Absalom's death – 18:16,17? (Think: How was Absalom's death a benefit to everyone else involved?)

12. What had Absalom done as a monument, and what reason did he give – 18:18? (Think: What does this tell us about Absalom?)

13. Who was Ahimaaz, and what request did he make – 18:19,20? How did Joab respond? (Think: What role had Ahimaaz had earlier in the story?)

14. Who carried the news instead of Ahimaaz – 18:21? What did Ahimaaz do then – 18:22,23? What success did he have?

15. Where was David, and what news was given him – 18:24,25? What did David conclude?

16. What did the watchmen say then, and what did David say – 18:26?

17. What report did Ahimaaz give to David – 18:27,28?

18. What question did David ask, and how did Ahimaaz respond – 18:29,30?

19. What message did the Cushite report – 18:31,32?

20. How did David respond to the news about Absalom – 18:33?

21. *Special Assignment:* Death of a child is naturally a time of grief, but was David's response here wise and proper? Explain.

Assignments on 2 Samuel 19

Read 2 Samuel 19, then answer the following questions.

1. What did the people hear about David, and how did this affect the victory – 19:1,2?

2. How is the conduct of the people described in 19:3,4?

3. What did Joab say the people had done for David but how had he treated them – 19:5?

4. How did he describe how David viewed Absalom compared to the people – 19:6? (Think: Was Joab's criticism valid? Explain.)

5. *Application*: What lessons should we learn about how we view the conduct of people who are close to us?

6. What did Joab tell David to do, and what would happen if he did not – 19:7?

7. So what did David do, and what did the people do – 19:8?

8. What dispute arose among the tribes of Israel – 19:9,10?

9. What message did David send to the priests – 19:11,12?

10. What other decision did David make recorded 19:13? What reason did he give?

11. **Special Assignment:** Why might this have been or not been a wise decision?

12. How did the men of Judah respond to David's message – 19:14,15?

13. What two men met David as he was returning – 19:16,17?

14. What confession and what request did Shimei make of David – 19:18-20? (Think: What wrong had Shimei done to David?)

15. **Application:** In what ways was Shimei's confession wise and in what ways was it not good?

16. What view did Abishai express regarding Shimei – 19:21?

17. What answer did David give to Abishai – 19:22? Explain his point.

18. What promise did David make to Shimei – 19:23? What punishment was later given (see cross-references)?

19. Who else met David – 19:24? How had he acted while David was gone?

20. What question did David ask him, and what answer did he give – 19:25-27? What accusation had Ziba made against him?

21. What request did Mephibosheth now make of David, and what reason did he give – 19:27,28

22. What verdict did David reach, and how did Mephibosheth respond – 19:29,30?

23. *Special Assignment:* Was David's decision fair? Explain your reasoning.

24. Who else met David at the Jordan – 19:31,32? What had this man done for David?

25. What offer did David make to him – 19:33?

26. How did Barzillai respond, and what reasons did he give – 19:34-36?

27. What request did Barzillai make, and what did David respond – 19:37,38?

28. Who then went with David across the Jordan, and who did not go – 19:39,40?

29. Who came to David, and what objection did they raise – 19:41?

30. What arguments did the two sides make for their claims – 19:42,43?

31. *Application*: Were the two sides reasonable in their arguments? What should we learn?

Assignments on 2 Samuel 20

Read 2 Samuel 20, then answer the following questions.

1. Who led the next revolt against David – 20:1? What claim did he make? Explain.

2. What did the men of Israel do, and what did the men of Judah do – 20:2?

> 3. **Special Assignment:** Describe the conflict that we have seen developing between Israel and Judah.

4. How did David treat the ten concubines that he had left in Jerusalem – 20:3? (Think: Why might he have treated them this way?)

5. What instruction did David give to Amasa? How did he fail – 20:4,5?

6. What concern did David have next – 20:6,7? What instruction did he give?

7. Where did Amasa meet the army, and how did Joab greet him – 20:8,9?

8. What did Joab do to Amasa then – 20:10?

> 9. **Special Assignment:** Summarize some of the good things Joab has done and some of the bad things he has done.

10. What was done with the body of Amasa and why – 20:11-13?

11. Where did Sheba seek refuge (see **map**) – 20:14?

12. What did Joab and his men do when they arrived – 20:15?

13. Who wanted to negotiate with Joab – 20:16,17?

14. How did she describe the reputation of her people – 20:18?

15. How did she describe herself, and what did she ask Joab – 20:19?

16. What explanation did Joab give for the attack, and what did he say would be required to end the siege – 20:21?

17. What agreement did the woman make, and what was the result when the people of the city did it – 20:21,22?

18. *Application*: What can we learn about the value of negotiation where people are willing to be peaceable?

19. Name the men who served under David and tell what position each one held. Where possible, give other information about them – 20:23-26.

Assignments on 2 Samuel 21

Read 2 Samuel 21, then answer the following questions.

1. What problem did Israel face, and what explanation did God give – 21:1?

2. Who were the Gibeonites, and what error had Saul committed regarding them – 21:2? (Think: What else do we read about them?)

3. What question did David ask of these people – 21:3?

4. What did the Gibeonites say they did not want – 21:4?

5. What request did they make – 21:5,6?

6. Whom was David determined not to give to the Gibeonites – 21:7? Why?

7. What men were given to the Gibeonites – 21:8,9?

8. What was done to the men – 21:9

9. What did Rizpah do for her sons – 21:10,11? Where else have we read about her?

10. Where were the bones of Saul and Jonathan at this time, and how had they gotten there – 21:12?

11. What did David do with the remains of Saul and his sons who had been slain – 21:13,14? What was the end result?

12. **Special Assignment:** Try to explain why God would consider Israel's oath to the Gibeonites to be binding considering the circumstances under which it had been made.

13. **Special Assignment:** In light of passages like Deuteronomy 24:16, why would God accept the death of Saul's descendants as punishment for the death of the Gibeonites?

14. Against whom was David fighting in 21:15-17? Who attempted to kill David?

15. Who protected David, and what did David's men determine as a result?

16. What battle was fought according to 21:18, and what victory occurred?

17. What conflict occurred in 21:19, and what victory occurred there?

18. Who fought for the Philistines according to 21:20? Describe him.

19. Who defeated him – 21:21?

20. What did four Philistines have in common in 21:22? (Think: Study the context and parallel passages and try to explain the relationship of the men.)

Workbook on 2 Samuel

Assignments on 2 Samuel 22

Read 2 Samuel 22, then answer the following questions.

1. Under what circumstances did David speak this song – 22:1?

2. List the expressions David used for God in 22:2,3. Explain the significance.

3. What did David do when facing enemies – 22:4? What was the result?

4. How did David describe his problems in 22:5,6?

5. How was God's response to David's prayer described in 22:7-9? Explain the significance.

6. *Application*: What lessons should we learn from David's description of God?

7. How is the coming of God described in 22:10,11? List other passages that may help explain the significance.

8. What is around God according to 22:12,13? Explain the contrast to verse 13.

9. How is God's voice described in 22:14,15? What happened when He spoke?

10. What problem is David described as having in 22:16,17? What did God do about it?

11. What benefit did David receive according to 22:18,19?

12. *Application*: Did God prevent David from suffering? What did He do for him? What should we learn from this?

13. Where did God bring David – 22:20? Explain the illustration.

14. What reason does David give to explain why God blessed him – 22:20-22?

15. How else does David describe his conduct in 22:23,24?

16. How did David's conduct affect God's treatment of him – 22:25?

17. For each of the following verses, describe how God treats various groups of people:
22:26 –

22:27 –

22:28 –

18. *Special Assignment:* Would God's treatment of people today be the same as His treatment of David and his enemies (physical blessings and military victory, etc.)? What is the difference and what should we learn?

19. How is God described in 22:29? List other *passages* using a similar illustration.

20. What did David say he could do according to 22:30? Can we do these things? Explain.

21. How is God described in 22:31,32? Why is this important to us?

22. How does David illustrate God's blessings in 22:33,34? Explain the illustration.

23. What did God provide for David in 22:35,36? What New Testament passage relates to this?

24. How is a large path better than a narrow path – 22:37?

25. Describe how David treated his enemies – 22:38-43? Should Christians treat their enemies physically this way? What is the lesson for us?

26. **Special Assignment:** Give examples elsewhere in which David's statements about himself were descriptions of the Messiah. In what ways might that be true in this case?

27. What had God done for David in relationship to his people – 22:44? Give examples.

28. What had God done for David in relationship to other nations – 22:44-46? In what sense might this be Messianic?

29. What is the significance of the fact that the Lord lives – 22:47? How does this contrast to heathen idols?

30. Once again, what does David say God does for him – 22:47-49?

31. What did David do because of God's blessings – 22:50? Where is this quoted in the New Testament, and what use does Paul make of it?

32. How does David conclude his song in 22:51?

Assignments on 2 Samuel 23

Read 2 Samuel 23, then answer the following questions.

1. How is David described in 23:1?

2. *Application*: What can we learn about direct inspiration from 23:2?

3. What instruction did God give rulers in 23:3? What should rulers learn from this?

4. To what is a good ruler compared in 23:4?

5. What did David say God had done for him in 23:5?

6. What messianic application would this have?

7. In contrast to a good ruler, how does David describe a rebel in 23:6,7? Explain.

8. Which of David's mighty men is described in 23:8, and what had he done?

9. What had another of David's mighty men done according to 23:9,10?

10. Who had accomplished a great victory according to 23:11,12? What had he done?

11. Where was David and where were the Philistines in 23:13-15 (see **map**)?

12. What wish did David express?

13. What did three mighty men do then – 23:16,17?

14. What did David do with the water, and what explanation did he give?

15. Who is described in 23:18,19, and what did he do?

16. What mighty man is described in 23:20-23, and what had he done?

17. 23:24-39 lists other of David's great warriors. Choose at least four of them and describe what information we know about them here or elsewhere.

Assignments on 2 Samuel 24

Read 2 Samuel 24, then answer the following questions.

1. What did God do and why according to 24:1?

2. ***Special Assignment:*** The parallel in 1 Chronicles says Satan moved David. How can this be harmonized with 2 Samuel? (Hint: Does God ever use Satan to accomplish His purposes?)

3. How did Joab respond to David's instruction – 24:2,3? (Think: What may have been wrong with David's instruction?)

4. Describe the route taken by those who numbered Israel in 24:4-7. Locate some of the places named (see **map**).

5. How long did the census take, and what was the end result – 24:8,9?

6. How did David react afterwards – 24:10?

7. ***Special Assignment:*** Describe what we learn once again about David's character.

8. Whom did God send to David, and what three choices was he offered – 24:11-13?

9. What reason did David give for his choice in 24:14?

10. What happened as result – 24:15?

11. What command did God give to the angel, and where was the angel – 24:16?

12. What plea did David make then – 24:17?

13. What command was David given then – 24:18?

14. What question did Arauna ask, and what answer did David give – 24:19-21?

15. What offer did Arauna make to David – 24:22,23?

16. What answer did David give, and what was his reason – 24:24?

17. List *passages* about sacrifices that we offer to God.

18. *Application*: What lessons should David's example teach us about the sacrifices that we offer to God?

19. What did David do, and what was the result – 24:25?

20. What other information are we given in 1 Chronicles 21:18-22:1 that relates to the same location?

Printed books, booklets, and tracts available at
www.gospelway.com/sales
Free Bible study articles online at
www.gospelway.com
Free Bible courses online at
www.biblestudylessons.com
Free class books at
www.biblestudylessons.com/classbooks
Free commentaries on Bible books at
www.biblestudylessons.com/commentary
Contact the author at
www.gospelway.com/comments
Free e-mail Bible study newsletter at
www.gospelway.com/update_subscribe.htm

Made in the USA
Middletown, DE
02 December 2021

53991100R00038